Fading Echoes, Rising Light

An Eclectic Collection of Poems

J.D. Terry

BookLeaf Publishing
India | USA | UK

Made with ❤ on the BookLeaf Publishing Platform
www.bookleafpub.in
www.bookleafpub.com

Dedication

This collection is dedicated to my mother, an English and Literature teacher of over 30 years.

Preface

In the quiet spaces between moments, there are stories that need to be told—stories of light and shadow, of growth and decay, of joy and sorrow. This collection of poems is a journey through the rawness of the human experience, an exploration of the delicate balance between darkness and light. Each poem captures the subtle yet profound reflections on nature, the heart, and the soul.

From the cycles of the seasons to the turmoil within, these verses echo the timeless truths of imperfection, loss, and resilience. They speak of the power of silence, the unspoken words that linger between us, and the whispers of hope that guide us through the storm. The beauty of nature—both its fury and its serenity—mirrors the chaos and peace we find within ourselves. There is a sense of longing and discovery in these words, a search for understanding, for connection, and for meaning in the face of an ever-changing world.

The poems invite you to sit with your own thoughts, to reflect on the quiet spaces of your heart, and to find comfort in the idea that we are never truly alone. As you turn these pages, you may recognize parts of your own story in these lines—parts of joy, sorrow, growth, and wonder. For at the core of it all, we are all bound by the same threads of emotion, ever-changing, ever-growing, ever-searching.

May this collection serve as a reminder that beauty exists in imperfection, strength in vulnerability, and light in even the darkest of nights.

Acknowledgements

I would like to thank my wife and son for being patient with me while writing this, and my mother for giving me a love of literature in all forms.

Day 1. A Passage of Time

The current is slow,
the river wide and smooth as glass.
It stretches out beneath the ship—
high above, we stand in safety.
The dewy morning sun
sparkles like a million crystals.
This is a day to celebrate each year—
the birth of something new.

Now the dew has vanished.
The current quickens,
the glassy surface stirs with ripples.
The deck grows warm beneath our feet.
People fill the ship,
and the banks come alive with motion.
The sun climbs high,
revealing a world of open doors.
Now is the time to explore.
We stop at many ports beneath this brilliant light—
and at one called *Love*,

we board a smaller ship,
meant only for a few.

The sun begins to set.
The river narrows,
its speed increasing once again.
A golden glow bathes the port
where we left the large, safe vessel behind.
Love carries us forward
through swift and winding waters,
nimble enough to weave past every rock,
so long as the crew does their part.
The old ship could never have made it here.

Night draws near.
The river churns, speeding like time itself.
Some crewmates depart,
seeking ships of their own—
some vast and ocean-bound,
some built for quiet streams.
Only two remain.
We press on, searching for new ports.
Darkness falls.
We no longer see the river's path.
The current rages,
our small ship trembling beneath us.
Engines failing,

we hold on tight.
Stars glimmer faintly overhead,
while distant horns echo warnings.
Fog rolls in,
and the river is blind.
We cling to one another
as the ship careens from rock to rock.
Suddenly, the river widens,
and the current softens.
Maybe—just maybe—
there's hope in this long night.
The stars fade.
Silence settles.
Time holds its breath.
I remember the morning.
I remember all that came before.
So much passed,
so quickly.
If only the safety of the great ship were still near—
everything would be all right.
But a new sound rises—
rushing water.
The current surges again.
Racing to the deck,
the first mate stumbles—
and is gone,
swallowed by darkness.

The river shows no mercy.
It widens,
roars louder than thought.
The captain stands alone,
wishing he had never left the larger ship.
A crash.
The vessel jerks.
Water drowns all sound.
No stars.
No answers.
Where is the first mate?
The ship teeters on the edge.
What comes next is unknowable.
Darkness.
Silence.
The motors are dead.
The river takes command.
The ship falls.

A glowing sunrise greets the captain
on a new, high, safe ship.
The current is slow, gentle, smooth.
A new day on the river begins.

Day 2. A Walk Through a Forgotten City

We walk along a dim, narrow street,
its edges lined with large, weathered statues—
off-white marble now dulled by age.
They were once bright, smooth, full of purpose.
I try to picture them as they once were,
imagining the hands that carved each fold of stone,
the hearts that dreamed they'd last forever.
Time, of course, had other plans.

Further down this dark, damp path,
a faint floral scent mingles with the must of wet earth.
It drifts from just around the corner—
an ancient fragrance of decay and bloom.
Then, as if summoned,
a towering cathedral reveals itself from behind the mist.
Majestic. Silent. Almost invisible until now.
How could something so grand hide so well?
As we inch closer, step by step,
the aroma grows stronger—

thick with moss, flowers, memory.
Vines of impossible size twist and tangle
across the western wall,
obscuring slivers of stained-glass saints
trapped in frozen color.
Their holiness forgotten beneath the wisteria's reach.
If only someone could peel back the green
and see what once was.
But no one remains.

We move on, past the silent cathedral,
down another street slick with rain.
Moss outlines the cobblestones like old ink on a faded map.
Shuttered windows stare blankly from homes and shops,
each one caving inward with age.
What happened here?
Did time unravel it all,
or did the people simply vanish?
There is no certain answer.
Time does what it will.

And yet—there's beauty in what has been lost.
A different kind of beauty.
Though this place is abandoned,
it has become something new:
a quiet complexity no human hand could plan.

Nature reclaims its throne—
the statues, now eroded and streaked,
stand like sentinels of a forgotten age.
The vines bloom bolder than ever,
bright against the gray.
Perhaps the past is hard to see in this light,
but something else has emerged—
a strange, antique grace
that could only have come
by first being forgotten.

Day 3. On Grief

I was wearing a smile today
It has been so long
I haven't seen you if forever
I wish you hadn't gone

But I'm left with a shadow, hiding in each corner,
Whispering softly when silence gets warmer.
Creeping and lurking,
Ever so near,
Closer and closer, feeding my fear.

Then the room goes from bright to dark
It breaks my heart
I know where this is headed without a glance
There is emptiness in abundance
I wish I could escape
As the shadow grows it engulfs my thoughts
And leaves me speechless
Wanting to scream Why
I wasn't prepared for you to die

Memories fade of that fateful day
where we left you in the bed where you lay

In echoes of laughter, we play in the sun,
Now silence surrounds me, a battle lost, never won.
Your voice, a safe and soft melody that lingers still,
Yet fades like a sunset, against my will.

I trace the outlines of moments we shared,
But the weight of your absence feels too much to bear.
With every tear that falls, I stitch up the seams,
Mending my heart with the fabric of dreams.

So I wear this smile, a fragile disguise,
The mask of my grief, hiding the cries.
But deep in my soul, I'll carry you near,
In shadows and light, dad, you'll forever be here.

Day 4. Secrets in the Ocean

Beneath the waves, where light dares not go,
Secrets lie in the depths, shrouded, untold.
The calm surface betrays what lies below,
Shipwrecks of choices, stories drowned long ago.

In dark caves and shadows, where silence prevails,
Ancient treasures and bones tell forgotten tales.
The ocean, so vast, hides both calm and storm,
A mirror of the mind, where past lives are reborn.

The stillness above masks the chaos beneath,
A tempest of memories buried in the reef.
Each wave that crashes, each breeze that sighs,
Whispers of truths that the ocean denies.

For deep in its chest, where the cold currents twist,
Lies the unknown, a dark, lingering mist.
The ocean keeps them, hidden from sight,
As if to remind us of the darkness of night.

So we sail on, with hearts full of fear,
Chasing the surface, yet wishing to disappear.
For the deeper we dive, the more we may find,
The ocean holds all—our past and our mind.

Day 5. Motherhood as Seen by a Son

I remember her hands first—
always warm, always moving.
They held spoons and socks,
my fevered brow,
and sometimes,
the weight of the world.
I didn't see it then.

Mornings smelled like toast or waffles
She'd tie my shoes,
pack my lunch,
kiss my forehead like it was a shield.
I thought that's what mothers did—
and maybe they do—
but none did it quite like her.

Even tired, she hummed,
folding clothes like prayers,
whispering strength into cotton and thread.

At night,
she'd brush my hair with her fingers,
like she was brushing away the day.

The next morning,
my favorite pancakes were waiting.
As I grew,
I pushed.
I broke rules,
broke her heart once or twice.
But she never broke.
She stood like the house she made—
quiet, sturdy,
weathering me like wind.

Now I watch her with my son—
those same hands,
still soft,
still sure.
And I finally understand
what I couldn't back then:
that love,
real love,
isn't loud or showy—
it's a lifetime of showing up.

Day 6. The Background Friend

The room is full—too full to breathe,
With voices loud and hearts that leave.
Laughter spills from wall to wall,
But none of it will catch my fall.

I stand beside, but not within,
A smile I wear stretched paper-thin.
They're talking close, their eyes alight—
While mine drift somewhere out of sight.

I'm the one they call when plans fall through,
The extra chair, the safety crew.
A name they know, a face they trust—
But only when the night's a bust.

Glasses clink and stories spin,
But not one thread will let me in.
I nod, I laugh, I play the part,
While hiding holes inside my heart.

Too much sound, yet I'm unheard,
Surrounded, but without a word.
A "maybe next time," kind of friend—
The one they text but never send.
I wish someone would really see—
Not just the calm they get from me.

But lights stay bright, the music swells,
And I remain in private hells.
They see the shape, they hear my name,
But never ask beneath the frame.
So I just drift from room to room,
A background soul who leaves too soon.

Day 7. Future Self

Do you smile at the dreams we once held tight?
Have we found the peace we longed for each night?
Do you remember the times we felt lost,
And all the battles we fought, no matter the cost?
I hope we've learned how to be kind,
To love without fear, and leave doubt behind.

I hope we've built bridges to places unknown,
Not walls that keep us feeling alone.
Do you still carry the weight of old pain?
Or have you let it go, like flowers in rain?
Have you made room for joy, for love so true,
For laughter that feels like it's meant just for you?

Do you remember the vows we once spoke,
The promises made, each one a love's oath?
Is God still the anchor through dark and bright?
Holding us steady through every long night?

How is our son, the dream we once knew?

Does his laughter still fill the house
like a field covered morning dew?
Do his eyes still sparkle with every surprise,
As he learns from the world, and his spirit flies?

When life gets heavy, do you still recall
The strength that we had when we stood tall?
Has it burned into something that shines so bright,
Or does it hide quietly out of sight?

I hope we've learned to forgive and to heal,
To accept all the parts we once tried to conceal.
Have we found peace with the things that we've done,
And learned to embrace all that we've become?

And when we meet, years down the line,
I hope we both laugh at how far we've climbed.
That we've learned to hold on to what's true,
And let go of the things that no longer serve you.
I hope we've found our way, through all the strife,
And built a home filled with love and life.

Day 8. The Seasons of the Soul

Spring awakens the heart, soft and new,
Summer burns with passion, wild and true.
Autumn whispers of wisdom and letting go,
Winter is quiet, a pause before we grow.
Each season a step in the journey we take,
A cycle of change, for our souls to remake.
We shed and we bloom, we falter and rise,
Time etches its truth in our hearts and skies.
In the dance of the seasons, we find our whole
The ever-turning mirror of the soul.

The winds may shift, the skies may weep,
Yet within the storm, our roots run deep.
Through joy and sorrow, loss and grace,
We learn to move at life's own pace.

For though the years may weather our frame,
The fire within burns just the same.

And as we walk through time's wide door,
We carry each season, forevermore.

Day 9. Dreams

In the quiet sleep, we dream of what could be,
A world where everything flows, free.
But when we wake, all that remains is but a trace,
Faint echoes in the mind, a forgotten place.
Dreams are shadows, they linger in light,
Fading as the morning steals the night.
Yet sometimes a dream will return and stay,
A whisper that guides us through the day.
Not all is lost in the sun's harsh gleam—

For life itself begins with a dream.
They slip through the cracks of conscious thought,
Fragments of meaning we never quite caught.
A door half-open, a voice without face,
A timeless ache we cannot place.

Still they shimmer, just out of reach.
We chase them still, though they drift and blur,
Like smoke on wind or a vanished stir.
And in that chase, we come to see—

Our dreams are seeds of who we might be.
They bloom in silence, then slip away.

So hold them close, though they fade at dawn,
They are the maps we travel on.
For in their glow, both fierce and slight,
We find our purpose, born of night.
And trace their light through each new day.

Day 10. Technology and Humanity

We are connected by wires, yet somehow still alone,
Faces flicker on screens, but the touch we crave is far from home.
We build a world of glass and code, but forget the warmth of flesh and soul,
In the digital age, we seek connection, yet feel the void of isolation's toll.

We scroll for love, but feel the cold.

We post and share, yet hide what's real,
Wrapped in pixels, we forget to feel.
A thousand likes, but still we yearn,
For eyes that meet, for hearts that burn.

Behind the screen, we ache for more.

Still hope lives in each glowing frame,
In words that heal, in voices that name.

The human spark still pulses through—
Beyond the static, we break through.

And learn again what touch is for.

Day 11. Imperfect

The crack in the vase is where the light shines through,
The faded colors of an old photograph, too.
The rough-hewn stone, worn smooth by time,
Tells a story of struggle, of rhythm and rhyme.
In brokenness, we find a grace—
A dance of flaws, an honest place.

The chipped mug holds memories of tea,
Each imperfection a part of me.
The weathered pages of a book we've read,
Its torn edges speak of words unsaid.
In every dent and every tear,
Lives a tale that's precious, dear.

The scars on the skin, the lines on the face,
A map of moments, of love and of grace.
Each wrinkle tells a different story,
Of laughter, of sorrow, of fleeting glory.
These marks, they show the years well spent,
The beauty of time, the love it lent.

The crooked tree, its branches spread wide,
A symbol of strength, of standing with pride.
No need for perfection, no need to conform,
For in its flaws, it weathers the storm.
Imperfection is not to be feared—
It's where true beauty is revered.

The melody of life is not in the tune,
But in the pauses, the rhythm that swoons.
The missed notes and the out-of-key parts,
Are what make the music speak to our hearts.
For it's in the flaws, both loud and soft,
That we find our song, our voice aloft

So let the cracks show, let the edges fray,
For in the imperfection, we find our way.
It's not in perfection we find our grace,
But in the moments we embrace the space.
For beauty lives in what's not whole—
In imperfection, we find our soul.

Day 12. Nature's Fury

The sky darkens with a silent breath,
Whispers of danger, a harbinger of death.
Clouds twist and coil, a storm begins,
A hurricane's fury, where chaos spins.
The earth holds its breath—what comes next?

Winds howl like wolves in a fevered chase,
The ocean rises, a wild embrace.
Trees bow low in fearful dance,
Caught in nature's violent trance.
The world shivers, the storm draws near.

The waters rage, the heavens split,
The hurricane's grip, unyielding, fit.
The ground trembles as walls are breached,
The fury of nature, no peace reached.
In nature's rage, we are mere dust.

And then, the calm—heavy and deep,
A silence that swallows the world to sleep.

The storm has passed, but what remains?
A world reshaped by nature's chains.
We walk forward, with unknown eyes.

Day 13. Memories

I remember the smell of fresh-cut grass,
The warmth of summer that never could last.
Small hands held tight to the world,
As the days spun by, bright and unfurled.
A golden time without regret.

Laughter filled the air like a song,
And in those moments, we belonged.
Running barefoot, wild and free,
Climbing dreams like every tree.
A world not ready to forget.

Now echoes live in distant sounds,
In old backyards and hometown grounds.
But in my heart, they still reside—
Those sunlit days I keep inside.
A sacred past I carry yet.

Now the years are folded, like pages in a book,
But I can still hear the rustle if I take a look.

The days may fade, but they live in my heart,
A place where memories never depart.
Forever young, though time may take its toll.

Day 14. A Day in the Life of a Tree

I stand still as the world moves fast,
Seasons come and go, they never last.
Birds rest on my branches, the winds whisper through my leaves,
And I watch as life unfolds before me, rooted, patient, timeless.
The sky is my story, the soil my song.

Children once carved their names in my bark,
Lovers kissed beneath me long after dark.
I've listened to laughter, to sorrow and rain,
To the hush of snow and the buzz of a train.
Each echo a part of the life I hold.

I do not wander, yet I see all things—
Storms, new births, and wedding rings.
The years move past in rings of grain,
In stillness, I've learned joy and pain.
Time does not rush where roots run deep.

At dusk, the sky folds into flame,
And still I stand, unchanged in name.
When morning comes, I'll stretch once more—
And greet the wind with an ancient lore.
This is enough. This is life.

Day 15. Unspoken Words

There are words I never said, a silence that lies heavy between us,
It hangs in the air like smoke, the unspoken, a quiet ache.
What could have been is lost in the gaps of our conversations,
The weight of silence, a story untold, a lingering sensation.
We build walls with unspoken thoughts,
Our hearts beat, but the distance is caught.

The spaces between us speak louder than the words we dared not say,
A dance of gestures, glances, half-finished phrases swept away.
What we meant to voice gets lost in the ebb of time,
Where hesitation blooms in the cracks of our rhyme.
Each pause, a riddle we failed to unfold,
The silence a language both soft and cold.

Now, we stand on the edge of what we never shared,
Two souls adrift, with a gap that's too wide, yet rare.
For in our silence, we find both grief and grace,
A tenderness buried in what's left unspoken in this space.
But maybe silence is the answer we seek—
A truth in its quiet, a solace unique.

Day 16. The Sacrifice

Emotions of Jesus on Calvary
are a mystery to me,
how he could forgive
those who took his life.

I cannot fathom
the depth of his love,
how he willingly gave himself up
to save us all.

But perhaps the greatest sacrifice
was not on the cross,
but in the garden of Gethsemane,
where he prayed for this cup to pass.

He knew what was to come,
the pain, the betrayal, the agony.
Yet still, he submitted to God's will,
for the sake of our salvation.

And so I bow my head in reverence
and give thanks for his sacrifice,
for without it, I would be lost,
but with it, I am found.

Day 17. Home

Home was the soft hum of her voice,
A lullaby woven from years of love and sacrifice.
It was the warmth in the kitchen,
The scent of her hands in flour,
The way she held the world without saying a word.
Her love was the gravity that kept the earth steady,
Her smile the place where everything began.
Home was her arms—always open, always steady.

But now, home is the way my own child laughs,
The way the little feet echo down the hall,
The quiet moments when we sit together,
The unspoken bond in a glance shared over dinner.
It's in the messy drawings on the fridge,
The sound of his voice filling the air,
And in the moments when he crawl into bed with me,
Seeking warmth, seeking love, seeking the same thing I once did.
Home is the innocence, the joy, the wildness—
A new kind of love, a new kind of gravity,

And it spins, as it always has, in circles of joy.

In his eyes, I see my mother,
And in my hands, I hold them like she once held me—
A cycle of tenderness passed down, unbroken.
Home, I realize, is not a place—it's a feeling,
A pulse that beats across generations,
A steady rhythm that whispers,
You are safe here, you are loved here,
You belong here.

Day 18. The Sky at Night

The stars are whispers in the dark,
a canvas of light, a quiet spark,
The moon watches, steady and true,
as the night sky unfolds in hues of blue.
We are but fleeting, but the sky remains,
a reminder of all that is infinite,
A vast expanse of wonder, where dreams and reality
intertwine,
delicate and intimate.
A lullaby written in celestial ink.

Each star a story, ancient and bright,
Burning in silence, refusing the night.
The cosmos speaks without a sound,
In turning worlds that know no bound.
And in their glow, we pause to think.

We make wishes we may not recall,
We name constellations that never fall.
But something in the sky feels near,

Like distant love that's always here.
It listens more than we might know.

The milky way swirls like a river of light,
Flowing through shadows, guiding the night.
It hums a song we can't quite hear,
Yet our hearts understand, far and near.
A melody born from stars, untold.

The planets turn in their endless dance,
Spinning in rhythm, lost in trance.
They carry secrets in their wake,
Stories of time, of love, of fate.
Each orbit a promise never broken.

And in the stillness, we find our place,
Small yet sacred in this vast space.
The sky holds us, and we hold it too—
Bound by dreams, both old and new.
Forever connected, by stars unspoken.

Day 19. A Myth Reimagined

Icarus wears earbuds now, his wings lit by LED,
He scrolls through skies of curated feeds,
still flying too close to what burns.
Pandora taps her screen—and the last hope flickers,
pixelated,
Ancient tales reborn, modern myths created.
Our gods wear brands, our monsters trend.

Medusa stares from viral posts,
Her gaze now captions and digital ghosts.
Narcissus streams in a selfie haze,
Lost in loops of endless praise.
And Echo replies with auto-send.

But still, beneath the filtered screen,
The old truths live, unseen, serene.
The thirst for more, the cost of pride—
These stories still walk by our side.
History rewound, again to bend.

Prometheus hacks the firewall flame,
Steals code not fire, but just the same.
He's chained to lawsuits, endless scrolls,
Paying the price for feeding souls.
The light we crave comes with a cost.

Aphrodite filters love through apps,
She swipes through hearts, but misses gaps.
Connection sold in dopamine pings,
Yet lonely still beneath the flings.
Desire has changed, but not the loss.

Athena blogs with wisdom's gaze,
But trolls still shout in foolish haze.
Her armor's words, her battle thought,
Yet even she feels overwrought—
A war of minds with no applause.

Hercules lifts at the gym for fame,
Twelve reps for likes, not quests or name.
His labors now are gains and views,
Still seeking worth he didn't choose.
Strength without meaning leaves a void.

We dress them new, but their hearts remain,
Woven in joy, in love, in pain.
Each tale reborn in a different guise,

Still asking questions, still telling lies—
Still warning us beneath the trend.

Day 20. What Once Was

They slip through the cracks of conscious thought,
Fragments of meaning we never quite caught.
A door half-open, a voice without face,
A timeless ache we cannot place.

Still they shimmer, just out of reach.
We chase them still, though they drift and blur,
Like smoke on wind or a vanished stir.
And in that chase, we come to see—
Our dreams are seeds of who we might be.
They bloom in silence, then slip away.

So hold them close, though they fade at dawn,
They are the maps we travel on.
For in their glow, both fierce and slight,
We find our purpose, born of night.
And trace their light through each new day.

Day 21. Return to the Maelstrom

What seems like the darkest night, every time,
In the morning, God paints a sunrise as He controls the light.
When the weight of despair feels too much to bear,
And thoughts spiral, tangled in endless despair,
He whispers through the silence, a gentle reminder,
That even the deepest shadows must surrender to light.

In the silence of my mind, the echoes grow loud,
A storm inside, I lose myself in the crowd.
But even in chaos, a soft voice speaks true,
A reminder that storms, like shadows, are few.
With each breath, I find a flicker of peace,
And the grip of the darkness begins to cease.

In the chaos of my mind, where I lose my way,
I forget that dawn will come, and the night will decay.
But each morning, despite my doubts, a new hope appears,

A promise that the storm will pass, despite my fears.
God’s grace is the brush that paints my soul anew,
Each sunrise a reminder that I'm never alone, and
neither are you.